Jack C. Richards & Chuck Sandy

Passages

Third Edition

Workbook 2 B

CAMBRIDGE
UNIVERSITY PRESS

CAMBRIDGE
UNIVERSITY PRESS

32 Avenue of the Americas, New York, NY 10013-2473, USA

Cambridge University Press is part of the University of Cambridge.

It furthers the University's mission by disseminating knowledge in the pursuit of education, learning and research at the highest international levels of excellence.

www.cambridge.org
Information on this title: www.cambridge.org/9781107627802

© Cambridge University Press 2015

First published 1998
Second edition 2008

Printed in Hong Kong, China, by Golden Cup Printing Company Limited

A catalog record for this publication is available from the British Library.

ISBN 978-1-107-62707-9 Student's Book 2
ISBN 978-1-107-62714-7 Student's Book 2A
ISBN 978-1-107-62715-4 Student's Book 2B
ISBN 978-1-107-62726-0 Workbook 2
ISBN 978-1-107-62734-5 Workbook 2A
ISBN 978-1-107-62780-2 Workbook 2B
ISBN 978-1-107-62766-6 Teacher's Edition 2 with Assessment Audio CD/CD-ROM
ISBN 978-1-107-62749-9 Class Audio 2 CDs
ISBN 978-1-107-62773-4 Full Contact 2
ISBN 978-1-107-62774-1 Full Contact 2A
ISBN 978-1-107-62777-2 Full Contact 2B
ISBN 978-1-107-62764-2 DVD 2
ISBN 978-1-107-68650-2 Presentation Plus 2

Additional resources for this publication at www.cambridge.org/passages

Book design: Q2A / Bill Smith
Art direction, layout services and photo research: Tighe Publishing Services

Contents

Credits

Illustration credits

Jo Goodberry: 12
Paul Hostetler: 19, 26, 38, 49
Kim Johnson: 10, 31, 36, 55, 64
Dan McGeehan: 17, 18, 48
Koren Shadmi: 3, 20, 34, 43, 61
James Yamasaki: 41, 68

Photography credits

1 ©Photodisc/Thinkstock; **4** (*left to right*) ©Blend Images/Alamy, ©arek_malang/Shutterstock, ©Suprijono Suharjoto/Thinkstock; **5** (*clockwise from center left*) ©Fuse/Thinkstock, ©Michael Simons/Alamy, ©pcruciatti /Shutterstock, ©Dmitriy Shironosov/Thinkstock; **6** ©Catherine Yeulet/Thinkstock; **7** ©Fuse/ Thinkstock; **8** ©crystalfoto/Shutterstock; **13** ©ID1974/Shutterstock; **14** (*top to bottom*) ©Olena Mykhaylova/ iStock/Thinkstock, ©Oleksiy Mark/Thinkstock; **15** ©Stocktrek Images/Getty Images; **21** ©Flirt/SuperStock; **22** ©Photononstop/SuperStock; **23** ©BananaStock/Thinkstock; **24** ©ollyy/Shutterstock; **25** ©Khakimullin Aleksandr/Shutterstock; **27** (*top to bottom*) ©Vuk Vukmirovic/iStock/Thinkstock, ©Moviestore Collection Ltd/Alamy; **28** ©NBC/Getty Images; **30** ©CBS Photo Archive/Getty Images; **32** ©Larry Busacca/TAS/Getty Images; **35** ©Creatas/Getty Images/Thinkstock; **39** ©Cusp/SuperStock; **40** ©Tammy Hanratty/MediaBakery; **42** ©Photoshot/Hulton/Getty Images; **45** (*top to bottom*) ©Sergey Nivens/Shutterstock, ©iStock/ franckreporter, ©iStock/MachineHeadz; **47** (*left to right, top to bottom*) ©Dean Bertoncelj/iStock/Thinkstock, ©Universal/Courtesy: Everett Collection, ©Kylie McLaughlin/Lonely Planet Images/Getty Images, ©MariusdeGraf/Shutterstock, ©Blend Images/Masterfile, ©Gao lin hk/Imaginechina/AP Images; **50** (*left to right, top to bottom*) ©MustafaNC/Shutterstock, ©Dmitry Zinovyev/Shutterstock, ©e2dan/Shutterstock, ©Reinhold Leitner/Shutterstock, ©Reddogs/Shutterstock, ©Nailia Schwarz/Shutterstock, ©Sergey Goruppa/Shutterstock, ©Wendy Kaveney Photography/Shutterstock, ©Donovan van Staden/Shutterstock, ©Nantawat Chotsuwan/Shutterstock, ©Steve Byland/istock/Thinkstock, ©iStock/Sergey Goruppa; **52** ©KidStock/Blend Images/Corbis; **53** (*top to bottom*) ©Gary Crabbe/Enlightened Images/Alamy, ©Falk Kienas/istock/Thinkstock; **54** ©Eric Isselée/Thinkstock; **57** ©E+/MachineHeadz/Getty Images; **59** ©Assembly/Media Bakery; **62** (*left to right, top to bottom*) ©Pressmaster/Shutterstock, ©Olga Danylenko/ Shutterstock, ©iStock/btrenkel, ©Stockbyte/Thinkstock, ©Graham Oliver/Media Bakery, ©Andrey Yurlov/ Shutterstock; **63** © INTERFOTO/Alamy; **65** ©Jon Kopaloff/FilmMagic/Getty Images; **66** ©ZUMA Press, Inc./Alamy; **71** ©Goodluz/Shutterstock; **Back cover:** (*clockwise from top center*) ©Leszek Bogdewicz/ Shutterstock, ©Wavebreak Media/Thinkstock, ©Blend Images/Alamy, ©limpido/Shutterstock

Text credits

The authors and publishers acknowledge the following sources of copyright material and are grateful for the permissions granted. While every effort has been made, it has not always been possible to identify the sources of all the material used, or to trace all copyright holders. If any omissions are brought to our notice, we will be happy to include the appropriate acknowledgments on reprinting.

12 Adapted from "Decoding Body Language," by John Mole, 1999, http://www.johnmole.com. Reproduced with permission; **18** Adapted from "How Artificial Intelligence is Changing Our Lives," by Gregory M. Lamb. Adapted with permission from the September 16, 2012 issue of *The Christian Science Monitor*. Copyright © 2012 The Christian Science Monitor, www.CSMonitor.com; **24** Adapted from "Rumor Detectives: True Story or Online Hoax?" by David Hochman, *Reader's Digest*, April 2009. Reprinted with permission from Reader's Digest. Copyright © 2009 by The Reader's Digest Association, Inc.; **30** Adapted from an NPR news report titled "Is The 'CSI Effect' Influencing Courtrooms?" by Arun Rath, originally published on NPR.org on February 5, 2011 and used with the permission of NPR. Copyright © 2011 National Public Radio, Inc. Any unauthorized duplication is strictly prohibited; **36** Adapted from "Study Suggests Music May Someday Help Repair Brain," by Robert Lee Hotz, *Los Angeles Times*, November 9, 1998. Copyright © 1998 Los Angeles Times. Reprinted with permission; **42** Adapted from "What's the Tipping Point?" by Malcolm Gladwell. Copyright © by Malcolm Gladwell. Reprinted by permission of the author; **48** Adapted from "Sensory Ploys and the Scent of Marketing," by Robert Budden, *Financial Times*, June 3, 2013. Copyright © The Financial Times Limited 2013. All Rights Reserved; **54** Adapted from "Fairy Tale Comes True," by Alexandar S. Dragicevic, *The Toronto Star*, July 23, 1998. Copyright © Associated Press; **60** Adapted from "Does the Language you Speak Change the Way You Think?" by Kevin Hartnett, *The Boston Globe*, February 27, 2013. Reproduced with permission of Kevin Hartnett; **66** Adapted from "Tiny Grants Keep 'Awesome' Ideas Coming," by Billy Baker, *The Boston Globe*, October 10, 2011. Copyright © 2011 Boston Globe. All rights reserved. Used by permission and protected by the Copyright Laws of the United States. The printing, copying, redistribution, or retransmission of this Content without express written permission is prohibited; **72** Adapted from "The Twelve Attributes of a Truly Great Place to Work," by Tony Schwartz, *Harvard Business Review*, September 19, 2011. Reproduced with permission.

7 CHANGING TIMES
LESSON A ▶ *Lifestyles in transition*

1 GRAMMAR

Underline the relative pronouns in this announcement.

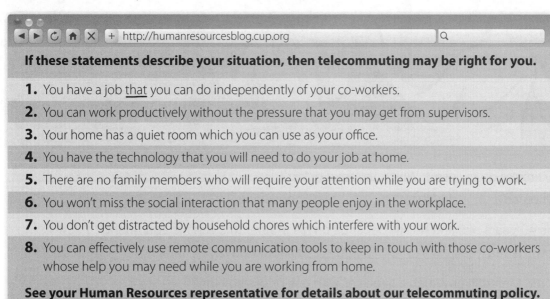

http://humanresourcesblog.cup.org

If these statements describe your situation, then telecommuting may be right for you.

1. You have a job <u>that</u> you can do independently of your co-workers.

2. You can work productively without the pressure that you may get from supervisors.

3. Your home has a quiet room which you can use as your office.

4. You have the technology that you will need to do your job at home.

5. There are no family members who will require your attention while you are trying to work.

6. You won't miss the social interaction that many people enjoy in the workplace.

7. You don't get distracted by household chores which interfere with your work.

8. You can effectively use remote communication tools to keep in touch with those co-workers whose help you may need while you are working from home.

See your Human Resources representative for details about our telecommuting policy.

2 GRAMMAR

Combine these sentences using a relative pronoun. Then write *O* if the relative pronoun is optional and *R* if the relative pronoun is required.

_*O*_ 1. Physical fitness is an important goal. A lot of people try to achieve this goal.

    Physical fitness is an important goal that a lot of people try to achieve.

_____ 2. Many people stay fit. These people find the time to work out regularly at a gym.

_____

_____ 3. For the best results, it's important to find a gym. You like this gym.

_____

_____ 4. It may be a good idea to hire a trainer. A trainer can work with you privately.

_____

_____ 5. Your trainer can give you advice. The advice can help you avoid injuries.

_____

_____ 6. If you get bored at the gym, try bringing some music. You can listen to the music while you exercise.

_____

3 VOCABULARY

Use the words in the box to complete these conversations.

| consistent | illogical | immature | inconsiderate | indecisive | responsible |

1. A: I can't make up my mind. Which tie looks better?

   B: Don't be so _____ *indecisive* _____. Just choose one.

2. A: Jim is 40 years old, and he still depends on his mother to clean his apartment.

   B: I know. He really is _____ in some ways.

3. A: Why did Meredith buy such a large car with gas prices so high?

   B: I know it seems _____, but she needs a big car for her job.

4. A: Doesn't Allison look great? What is she doing?

   B: She's been eating better and exercising on a _____ basis.

5. A: Why does Nate play his music so loudly when he knows we have to study?

   B: I don't know. He's so _____ of our needs. He just doesn't care.

6. A: I really like the new waiter you hired. He's very dependable.

   B: Yes, he is. Even though he's young, he's quite _____.

4 GRAMMAR

Use relative clauses and your own ideas to complete these sentences.

1. I have always admired people *who are good at organizing their time.* _____

2. I've always thought that I would enjoy a lifestyle _____

3. Parents _____ should be greatly admired.

4. These days many people want jobs _____

5. Finding enough time to spend with family and friends is a problem _____

_____

5 WRITING

A Read this composition about a personal experience and answer the questions.

The family that eats together, stays together

I feel it is very important for families to have regular meals together. One of my most positive childhood memories was dinner with my parents and two sisters. As a result, last year I decided that my family would have dinner together three days a week. Because my husband and I both work, and our kids are busy with school activities, we found that we rarely had a chance to get together as a family. But we thought it would be possible for everyone to set aside three evenings a week for a sit-down dinner.

First, we tried setting three fixed days for our experiment – Mondays, Wednesdays, and Fridays. After a couple of weeks of trying this plan, almost everyone was unhappy. Then my son had the idea of having everyone post his or her schedule for the week on the refrigerator every Sunday. I would choose the three best days, and those with scheduling conflicts . . .

For a while, the kids continued to resist the idea. They said they would rather spend the time with their friends or participate in sports or other activities. Gradually, though, they began to see these evenings together in a very positive way. We laughed a lot. We made vacation plans. We discussed each other's problems. After a couple of months, anyone who had to miss a family meal felt . . .

We all feel that we have been able to build much stronger relationships within the family than we had before. Of course, there are still disagreements, but we communicate better with each other now. The idea of having regular family meals together, which seemed difficult at first, has brought about many positive changes in our lives.

1. What is the thesis statement?

   _____

2. What is the focus of the second paragraph?

   _____

3. What is the focus of the third paragraph?

   _____

4. What sentence in the conclusion restates the thesis statement?

   _____

B Write a thesis statement for a composition about an important decision you have made recently.

   _____

   _____

C Now write your composition. Include an introduction, two paragraphs providing background information and details, and a conclusion.

1 GRAMMAR

Choose the expressions that best complete the sentences.

1. Cathy has decided to give up her high-powered job and do something more personally satisfying *like* / *as though* several of her friends have done.

2. Doesn't it seem *the way* / *as if* more people are trying to live a simpler life?

3. Elena feels *as* / *as though* she spends too much of her time commuting, so she is looking for work that she can do from home.

4. Today's kids don't have a lot of free time, *as* / *as if* we did when we were growing up, but they have many more opportunities.

5. Schools should offer music and art *as if* / *the way* they did when I was a student.

6. *As* / *As though* my aunt always says, "Make new friends, but keep your old ones."

7. Some days I feel *as if* / *the way* time passes too quickly.

8. *Like* / *As though* my mother before me, I serve a traditional dinner on special holidays for my family to enjoy.

2 VOCABULARY

Choose the expressions that are best exemplified by each situation.

a. anticipate a change	c. cope with change	e. resist change
b. bring about a change	d. go through a change	f. welcome a change

_e_ 1. Sherri's friends want her to move to Los Angeles with them, but she keeps coming up with reasons why she shouldn't go.

_____ 2. Mr. Viera's ideas encouraged our company to find ways for employees to work more closely with other departments.

_____ 3. After being on a plane for eight hours, Eun-ju was happy to finally land in Hawaii and begin her vacation.

_____ 4. When Mark retired from his job, he started playing golf and volunteering at the food bank.

_____ 5. Our school is in the process of moving to a new building and revising the schedule, so it's a challenging time for everyone.

_____ 6. We've realized it's time to move to a bigger house. We plan to start looking for a new place next month.

GRAMMAR

Read each situation and answer the questions using *as if*, *as though*, *as*, or *the way*. Sometimes more than one answer is possible.

1. Cal used to look forward to going fishing with his sons every summer. Now, his sons don't have time to go anymore. How does Cal feel?

   He feels as if he has lost a
   family tradition.

2. Anna has moved from a small town to a big city. It's exciting, and she's meeting lots of new people and discovering many new activities. How does Anna feel?

   _____

3. Mia used to spend a lot of time with her grandmother. Since Mia moved away, she only sees her grandmother twice a year. How does Mia feel?

   _____

   _____

4. In his spare time, Chris took an art class and discovered he had a real talent. Now he's about to have his first show in a gallery. How does Chris feel?

   _____

   _____

GRAMMAR

Complete these sentences so that they are true for you. Use *as if*, *as though*, *as*, *the way*, and *like*.

1. I feel ____*as though social media*____ is changing the way I relate to my friends.

2. I don't feel _____

   _____ when I was younger.

3. These days I think many people act _____

4. I still _____

   _____ my family did years ago.

5. Some people my age talk _____

   _____

READING

A Read the interview with Malcolm Gladwell about his book *The Tipping Point*. Find the words in boldface that match the definitions.

1. sudden increases in the occurence of something unpleasant _____*outbreaks*_____

2. the scientific study of epidemics _____

3. a comparison of two similar things _____

4. easily spread _____

THE TIPPING POINT: Q & A with Malcolm Gladwell

1 What is *The Tipping Point* about? It's a book about change. In particular, it's a book that presents a new way of understanding why change so often happens as quickly and as unexpectedly as it does. For example, why did crime drop so dramatically in New York City in the mid-1990s? How does a novel written by an unknown author end up as a national bestseller? Why is word-of-mouth so powerful? I think the answer to all these questions is the same. It's that behavior and messages and products sometimes behave just like **outbreaks** of infectious disease. They are social epidemics. *The Tipping Point* is an examination of the social epidemics that surround us.

2 Do you think the epidemic example is relevant for other kinds of change? I'm convinced that ideas and behaviors and new products move through a population very much like a disease does. This isn't just a metaphor. I'm talking about a very literal **analogy**. Ideas can be **contagious** in exactly the same way that a virus is.

3 How would you classify *The Tipping Point?* Is it a science book? I like to think of it as an intellectual adventure story. It draws from psychology and sociology and **epidemiology**, and uses examples from the worlds of business and education and fashion and media . . . all in aid of explaining a very common but mysterious phenomenon that we deal with every day.

4 What do you hope readers will take away from the book? One of the things I'd like to do is to show people how to start "positive" epidemics of their own. The virtue of an epidemic, after all, is that just a little input is enough to get it started, and it can spread very, very quickly. That makes it something of obvious and enormous interest to everyone, from educators trying to reach students, to businesses trying to spread the word about their product, or for that matter, to anyone who's trying to create a change with limited resources. By the end of the book, I think the reader will have a clear idea of what starting an epidemic actually takes. This is not an abstract, academic book. It's very practical. And it's very hopeful. It's brain software.

B Read the interview again. Choose the statements that are true according to the text.

☐ 1. *The Tipping Point* is a nonfiction book that draws from a number of different fields.

☐ 2. Gladwell believes that ideas, messages, and products spread in similar ways.

☐ 3. Before writing the book, Gladwell started a social epidemic of his own.

☐ 4. According to Gladwell, social epidemics do not occur very often.

☐ 5. Gladwell believes *The Tipping Point* should appeal to a wide range of readers.

☐ 6. *The Tipping Point* is not meant to be a book with practical applications.

1 GRAMMAR

Underline the direct objects and circle the indirect objects in each sentence.

1. Some stores offer their (customers) frequent-buyer rewards as incentives to return.
2. Advertising is useful because it gives us information about improved products.
3. The salesperson recommended the latest headphones to me.
4. Someone had to explain the new printer to Daniel.
5. This GPS must have cost you a lot of money.
6. You should return those boots to the store if they're not comfortable.
7. Online auction sites offer collectors a great way to find the things they want.
8. I don't shop online often because I like to ask salespeople questions in person.

2 GRAMMAR

Unscramble the words to make sentences describing the woman's shopping experience.

1. the latest tablets / showed / the woman / the salesperson

    The salesperson showed the woman
    the latest tablets.

2. the woman / to / the GS5 model / recommended / the salesperson

    _____

3. her / the main features / he / described / to

    _____

4. him / the woman / the price / asked

    _____

5. the salesperson / the price / her / told

    _____

6. said / nothing / to / him / she / for a moment

    _____

7. a discount / offered / the salesperson / her

    _____

8. the money / the salesperson / she / to / gave

    _____

3 GRAMMAR

Use the words in the box to give advice about what to do in each situation. Include a direct and an indirect object in each sentence.

| lend | mention | recommend | return | teach |

1. Mai got a book from her brother for her birthday. She already has a copy of the book.
   Mai should return the book to the store and get one she doesn't have.

2. Ray and Pam want to go skiing with Kate, but Pam doesn't have enough money.
   _____

3. Ian speaks fluent Thai. His sister wants to learn Thai but doesn't want to take a class.
   _____

4. Jessica's favorite Italian restaurant is Luigi's. Her father wants to go out for Italian food but doesn't know any restaurants.
   _____

5. Max sold his car to a friend. The car uses a lot of oil, but he forgot to say anything about it.
   _____

4 VOCABULARY

Write a sentence about each situation using the expressions in the box.

| bargain hunter | compulsive shopper | shopping spree |
| buyer's remorse | credit limit | window-shopping |

1. Monica and Emil love to see what's on sale at their favorite stores. They can spend hours doing this without buying anything at all!
   Both Monica and Emil love to go window-shopping.

2. When Jeremy gets paid, he always buys things for himself whether he needs them or not. He often spends all of his money in one day.
   _____

3. Mark never pays full price for anything. He always searches for the best price. He even goes to different parts of town to get a good deal.
   _____

4. Before her wedding, Anne and her mother went shopping for everything they would need for the wedding. They spent a lot of money and had a great time.
   _____

5. Jen bought an expensive pair of earrings today. She loved them at the store, but now that she's home, she feels guilty for spending so much money.
   _____

6. While Eric was on vacation, he used his credit card for everything. At the end of the trip, he tried to buy a present, but his card was denied.
   _____

WRITING

A For each opinion, choose the two examples or details that support it.
Then write another sentence to support the opinion.

1. Using an online supermarket saves you time and money.

   ☐ a. Groceries purchased online are delivered directly to your home.

   ☐ b. There is less chance to make an impulse buy because you are not actually in the store.

   ☐ c. Online supermarkets often offer exotic produce that is not available in local grocery stores.

   _____

   _____

2. There is little reason to buy a camera if you have one on your phone.

   ☐ a. With the right apps, you can edit your photos on the phone and share them on social media.

   ☐ b. A good camera will usually produce better images than a phone.

   ☐ c. It's easy to forget to bring a camera, but you probably always have your phone with you.

   _____

   _____

3. Today's children are too materialistic.

   ☐ a. Many children have more free time than they have ever had before.

   ☐ b. They compete to have the coolest gadgets and the most expensive hobbies.

   ☐ c. Parents complain that children only want money from them.

   _____

   _____

B Write a thesis statement about one of the opinions above or one of your own.

_____

_____

C Write a composition. Include your thesis statement in the first paragraph, and develop your opinion with examples and details in subsequent paragraphs.

GRAMMAR

Read the email from a customer to the manager of a supermarket. Underline the subjunctive verbs.

Dear Manager,

I saw the sales flier for your supermarket, and I felt it was imperative that I <u>write</u> you. All the food on sale this week is snack food or other highly processed foods. Although I buy these foods occasionally, I suggest that local and organic foods be on sale, too. It's crucial that people have the chance to buy affordable local foods, and I recommend that your supermarket start offering these items at better prices. I also propose that you offer a larger selection of fresh fruits and vegetables. Many people don't buy fresh foods because they are not easily available. I think it's essential that your customers get the chance to incorporate these foods into their meals.

Thank you.

Marcella Guzman

GRAMMAR

Use the words in parentheses to rewrite each sentence using the subjunctive.

1. People should learn how to block offensive ads on their devices. (it is important)
   It is important that people learn how to block offensive ads on their devices.

2. A health-conscious person should eat fast food only once or twice a month. (it is vital)
   _____

3. Parents should read reviews before their children see a movie. (it is essential)
   _____

4. The government must prevent students from dropping out of school. (we insist)
   _____

GRAMMAR

Complete these sentences with your own ideas.

1. If you are suspicious about an ad for a product, I suggest that *you go online and read some reviews of the product.*

2. If you find an ad offensive, I recommend that _____

3. If you think a particular product is good, I propose that _____

4. If you want to pursue a career in advertising, it is important that _____

4 VOCABULARY

What marketing strategies would you use for each product or business? Use the phrases in the box to write sentences explaining your decisions.

celebrity endorsements	coupon codes	a loyalty program	search-engine marketing
comparative marketing	free samples	product placement	word-of-mouth marketing

1. ice cream *I would use free samples because everyone would taste the ice cream, and many people might like it so much they'd buy more.*

2. an action movie _____ _____ _____ _____

3. a new restaurant _____ _____ _____ _____

4. sports equipment _____ _____ _____ _____

5. a health club _____ _____ _____ _____

6. electronics _____ _____ _____ _____

A Read the article quickly. Which senses were the focus of the marketing strategies and experiments mentioned? Choose the correct answers.

☐ hearing   ☐ sight   ☐ smell   ☐ taste   ☐ touch

Sensory ploys and the scent of MARKETING

Global brands have become increasingly aware of the power of sight, smell, touch, and sound to influence purchasing behaviors.

A fast-food chain has trialed scents for use in its restaurants with the knowledge that this not only draws in customers but also improves their perception of their overall dining experience. A company that produces a popular deodorant for men has spent considerable sums perfecting the sound of its aerosol can to amplify its brand message of strength and effectiveness. This has led to a spray that is noticeably louder than their "female" deodorants.

A subtle scent or a particular sound can be just enough to awaken positive past associations or simply alter our other sensory perceptions. Charles Spence, professor of experimental psychology and a sensory consultant to brands, points to research conducted by a company about 15 years ago. The company discovered that by adding a fragrance to clothes, they were perceived by users as whiter even when they weren't.

Other tricks, such as using high-pitched music, can drive people toward the top of a website, Professor Spence says. Meanwhile, by simply changing the background color on their website, companies can increase trustworthiness. This is of particular value, for example, when asking customers to enter their credit card details.

But brands do not always get it right. Back in 2008, one food company knew that consumers responded positively not only to crunchier chips but also to noisier packaging. So it introduced new noisy packaging for one of its chips. It was so loud that it reached as high as 105 decibels, louder than a lawnmower or food processor. Two years later, the company withdrew the packaging following widespread consumer complaints. There can be advantages in tapping into consumers' senses, but brands can clearly go too far.

B Read the article again. Choose the correct answer for each question.

1. What is this article mostly about?
   ☐ a. How marketing improves consumers' sensory experience.
   ☐ b. How to avoid being tricked by sensory marketing strategies.
   ☐ c. How marketing makes use of the senses to influence consumers.

2. Which of these statements is true according to the article?
   ☐ a. Sensory information doesn't have to be obvious to affect our perception of a product.
   ☐ b. Sensory information only triggers positive associations.
   ☐ c. One sense has no influence on how the other senses perceive a product.

3. Which of the following is **not** mentioned in the article?
   ☐ a. Particular scents can drive consumers into a restaurant.
   ☐ b. A white product is considered more reliable by customers.
   ☐ c. Packages that produce the wrong sound can drive customers away.

9 NATURE

1 GRAMMAR

Complete these sentences using *whenever* or *wherever*.
If the time or place is specified, use *when* or *where*.

1. For some reason, _____*wherever*_____ I go with my pet snake, people get upset.

2. Many cats will rub against their owners' legs _____ they want to show affection.

3. Research indicates that _____ a person strokes an animal, his or her blood pressure goes down. Also, it's been argued that trained dogs should be present _____ there are people recovering from illnesses.

4. _____ I grew up, it wasn't common for people to have pets in their homes.

5. _____ I got my pet, I took on a serious responsibility. Being able to keep an animal healthy and fit depends on constant care and attention.

2 GRAMMAR

Rewrite the last sentence of each conversation with a sentence including a clause starting with *whenever* or *wherever*.

1. A: I'm going over to Chelsea's apartment. Would you like to come with me?
   B: No, I can't. She has a cat, and I'm allergic to them. Any time I'm around a cat, I start sneezing.
   Whenever I'm around a cat, I start sneezing.

2. A: Did you enjoy your visit to the rain forest preserve?
   B: I did. Everywhere I looked, there were amazing plants and animals.
   _____

3. A: What's wrong with your cat? She looks upset.
   B: She's just excited. She looks like that any time she sees a bird outside.
   _____

4. A: What kind of pet would you like to have?
   B: I'd love to get some fish. Any time I see fish swimming, I feel calm.
   _____

3 VOCABULARY

Write the correct word under each picture.

beak	fangs	fin	hooves	paws	tusks
claws	feather	gills	horns	tail	wing

1. _____feather_____

2. _____

3. _____

4. _____

5. _____

6. _____

7. _____

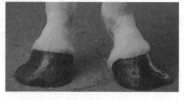
8. _____

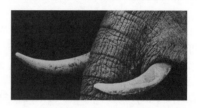
9. _____

10. _____

11. _____

12. _____

4 GRAMMAR

Complete these sentences so that they are true for you.

1. Whenever I spend time with animals, _____

   _____

2. When animals are kept in zoos, _____

   _____

3. Wherever there are performances by animals, _____

   _____

4. Wild animals should be kept where _____

   _____

 **WRITING**

A Read the thesis statements. Do the topic sentences belong in the composition? Choose yes or no.

	Yes	No
1. Thesis statement: Owning a pet has many health benefits.		
a. People who own pets often have better physical health than people who do not own pets.	☐	☐
b. People who own pets handle daily stresses better.	☐	☐
c. Pet owners often spend a lot of money on medicine for their pets.	☐	☐
d. People who have pets may be happier than other people.	☐	☐
2. Thesis statement: There are several effective ways to promote the survival of endangered animal species.		
a. Animals held in small enclosures often feel high levels of stress.	☐	☐
b. Conservation groups work to restore the natural habitats of endangered animals before reintroducing them to the wild.	☐	☐
c. Zoos are often successful at breeding endangered animals.	☐	☐
d. Hikers rarely spot endangered animals in the wild.	☐	☐
3. Thesis statement: Animal studies may lead to advances in technology.		
a. Spider web research could result in stronger buildings being built.	☐	☐
b. Learning more about how bats "see" in the dark may lead to new medical technologies.	☐	☐
c. Insects such as bees and ants live in highly structured societies.	☐	☐
d. Understanding how butterfly wings reflect light is inspiring engineers to create new types of computer screens.	☐	☐

B How are animals viewed in your culture? Write a thesis statement and topic sentences for three paragraphs.

Thesis statement: _____

_____

1. _____

2. _____

3. _____

C Now write a classification essay that includes your thesis statement in the introduction, three paragraphs corresponding to your topic sentences, and a conclusion.

GRAMMAR

Choose the words that best complete the sentences.

1. *Whatever /* (*Whoever*) has some free time this weekend should volunteer for the yearly beach cleanup.

2. Helen went to the woods to photograph *whatever / whoever* she could find for a project on medicinal plants.

3. The members of our surfing club are doing *whatever / whoever* they can to save enough for a trip to Hawaii.

4. I would never swim with sharks, but *whatever / whoever* does is very brave, in my opinion.

5. Can you tell me *whatever / whoever* you know about Professor Blake's research in the Arctic?

6. *Whatever / Whoever* has been dumping trash in the wildlife preserve should definitely be punished.

VOCABULARY

Complete the conversations with the correct idioms from the box.

a breath of fresh air	a walk in the park	the tip of the iceberg	set in stone
a drop in the ocean	as clear as mud	under the weather	up in the air

1. A: Do you understand these instructions?

   B: Not at all. They're _____ to me.

2. A: Are you feeling all right?

   B: Not really. I'm afraid I'm a little bit _____.

3. A: The new park director is full of great ideas!

   B: I know. She's _____ after working with the same people for so long.

4. A: I hear that the city spent way too much on the new waterfront park.

   B: Yes, but that's just _____. They overspent on many other projects, too.

5. A: Is it going to be difficult to raise money for the Save the Pandas campaign?

   B: I don't think so. They're such popular animals, it should be _____.

6. A: How closely do we have to follow the guidelines?

   B: They're not _____ yet, but let's keep them in mind while they're being finalized.

7. A: Have they decided who is going to speak at the biology convention in June?

   B: Not yet. It's still _____.

8. A: It's great that you're helping to save endangered owls.

   B: Unfortunately, it's just _____. There are many other animals that need help.

GRAMMAR

Do you agree or disagree with these statements? Respond to what the first speaker says. Write sentences with *whoever* or *whatever*.

1. A: It's acceptable to build resorts in protected natural areas.

   B: *I disagree. We should do whatever we can to protect natural areas.*

2. A: People who drop litter in parks should pay very large fines.

   B: _____

   _____

3. A: Everything governments usually do to protect endangered species is enough.

   B: _____

   _____

4. A: We should do everything we can to keep wild animals in their natural habitats.

   B: _____

   _____

5. A: People should never hike alone in unfamiliar forests.

   B: _____

   _____

BIRDS ONLY
Past This
Point

STATE OF CALIFORNIA
The Resources Agency
DEPARTMENT OF FISH AND GAME
Title 14, Section 630, CCR

GRAMMAR

Complete these sentences with ideas of your own. Use *whoever* or *whatever*.

1. *Whoever wants to have a real wilderness experience* should think about *trekking* *in the Australian outback.*

2. Whatever you need for your trip _____

   _____

3. _____

   must watch this nature documentary about _____

4. I do whatever I can _____

   _____

5. _____

   _____ will be amazed by the beautiful views.

A Read the title and first paragraph of this story, and answer the questions. Then read the rest of the story.

1. How well known is the fairy tale mentioned in the first paragraph? _____

2. What sentences indicate that the story will be true? _____

_____

A Fairy Tale Comes True

Every Bosnian child knows the story of a poor woman who caught a golden fish, released it, and in return gained wealth and happiness. It's a Balkan fairy tale, but it turned into reality for one poor family. "Whatever happened here is beyond good luck – it really is a fable," said Admir Malkoc.

In 1990, Smajo Malkoc returned from working in Austria to Jezero, a village surrounding a lake, in the former Yugoslavia. He had an unusual gift for his teenaged sons Dzevad and Catib: an aquarium with two goldfish.

Two years passed. War broke out, and Smajo Malkoc was killed.

When his wife, Fehima, sneaked back into the destroyed village to bury her husband, she spotted the fish in the aquarium. She let them out into the nearby lake. "This way they might be more fortunate than us," she recalls thinking.

Fast-forward to 1995. Fehima returned with her sons to Jezero to find ruins. Eyes misting over, she turned toward the lake and glimpsed something strange. She came closer – and caught her breath.

"The whole lake was shining from the golden fish in it," she said. During the years of war and killing all around the lake, life underwater had flourished.

After their return, Fehima and her sons started feeding the fish and then selling them. Now, homes, bars, and coffee shops in the region have aquariums containing fish from Jezero.

The Malkoc house, rebuilt from ruins, is one of the biggest in the village. The family says it has enough money not to have to worry about the future.

Other residents are welcome to catch and sell the fish. But most leave that to the Malkocs. "They threw the fish into the lake," said a villager. "It's their miracle."

B Put the events in order. Write an *X* for events not mentioned or indicated in the story.

_____ a. Mrs. Malkoc put the fish in a lake.

_____ b. The war broke out and Mr. Malkoc was killed.

_____ c. The Malkoc family started taking care of the fish in the lake.

_____ d. The Malkocs opened an aquarium in the village.

_____ e. Mrs. Malkoc and her children returned to their home.

_1_ f. Mr. Malkoc worked in another country.

_____ g. People from the region started buying fish from the Malkocs.

_____ h. The Malkocs provided money for other villagers to rebuild their homes.

_____ i. Mr. Malkoc presented two goldfish to his children when he came home.

GRAMMAR

Choose the words or phrases that best complete the sentences.

1. Kyle (*was giving*) / *was being given* a presentation in front of the whole company for the first time in his life.

2. When he *introduced* / *was introduced* by the vice president of the company, she got his name wrong.

3. When Kyle turned on the projector, everyone saw a family photo instead of the presentation that *should have displayed* / *should have been displayed* on the screen.

4. He was so flustered that he *dropped* / *was dropped* his tablet on the floor.

5. When he picked up the tablet, it *wasn't working* / *wasn't being worked*.

6. Kyle knew a copy of the presentation *might have saved* / *might have been saved* on his manager's tablet, so he borrowed it.

7. In spite of the initial problems, the presentation went well, and Kyle's manager *has praised* / *has been praised* him for a job well done.

GRAMMAR

Rewrite each sentence using the passive voice. Do not include the agent.

1. After the soccer team won the championship, the coach thanked the players.
   The players were thanked after the soccer team won the championship.

2. People have told me that I have good presentation skills.

   _____

3. Schools should teach foreign languages beginning in elementary school.

   _____

4. My college is awarding a new prize to the best debate team.

   _____

5. Someone is going to interview the best-selling author on TV tonight.

   _____

3 VOCABULARY

Rewrite the sentences by replacing the underlined words with a word or phrase from the box. If there are two possible answers, write both of them.

first of all	in addition	likewise	next	to begin	yet
furthermore	in conclusion	nevertheless	similarly	to sum up	

1. <u>To start with</u>, welcome to our seminar, "Giving Your Best Presentation."

   To begin / First of all, welcome to our seminar, "Giving Your Best Presentation."

2. When faced with giving a presentation, many people don't know where to start. <u>Also</u>, many of us get very nervous just thinking about presenting our ideas in public.

   _____

3. So, here are a few tips. <u>Before anything else</u>, outline your ideas carefully.

   _____

4. Make sure you have all the visuals you need for your presentation. <u>However</u>, don't depend too much on pictures and charts – what you say is just as important.

   _____

5. Don't rush the preparation of your materials. <u>In the same manner</u>, give yourself plenty of time to become familiar with the information you want to communicate.

   _____

6. <u>Then</u> practice the presentation a couple of times to build your confidence.

   _____

7. <u>To conclude</u>, preparation, practice, and confidence are the keys to a successful presentation.

   _____

4 GRAMMAR

Complete the sentences with your own ideas. Use the passive.

1. _My best friend's team was awarded_ first prize in the university debate competition.

2. _____

   _____ when he / she turned the radio up too loud in the car.

3. _____

   _____ he / she talks too much while watching movies.

4. _____

   _____ a speech at our school's graduation ceremony.

5. _____

   _____ for being one of the most generous people in our country.

A Read the two positions about whether or not schools should focus on teaching students how to do research online. Then find the supporting reasons for each position, and write them on the lines below.

Positions

1. Since knowing how to do research online is essential for twenty-first century learners, it should be focused on in schools.

_____

_____

_____

2. While knowing how to do research online is important for twenty-first century learners, it should not be a focus in schools.

_____

_____

_____

Reasons

• Most students in the twenty-first century already have the necessary skills to do research online or can learn these skills on their own.

• The Internet is changing rapidly, and the skills students learn today may no longer be relevant in the near future.

• Most students would benefit from training on how and where to find reliable information online.

• Learning how to successfully do research online is as important to future studies and careers as learning subjects such as math and history is.

• Class time should be used for teaching more complex content and skills.

• Many students need guidance to learn how to distinguish trustworthy sources from unreliable ones.

B Which position is closer to your own? Write a persuasive composition to explain your point of view. Be sure to argue against the opposing view.

GRAMMAR

Choose the correct form of the verbs. Sometimes more than one answer is possible.

At first, most social media sites **(1)** *was /*(*were*) seen as a fun way to keep in touch with friends, share photos, and play games. But anyone who **(2)** *uses / use* one of these websites today can see that many more important things **(3)** *is / are* going on, and no one using these sites regularly **(4)** *is / are* able to ignore the fact that their uses are changing. A lot of people **(5)** *shares / share* political news and information, and new ideas can start and grow on these sites. Also, if someone **(6)** *needs / need* help after an accident or disaster, social media can be used to spread the word. In some instances, a majority of the money raised for emergency situations **(7)** *comes / come* through social media, and many volunteers can be brought together in a matter of hours. Of course, none of us **(8)** *puts / put* our social media account to such serious uses all of the time, but it is great to know that the possibility is there if we need it.

GRAMMAR

Read these results from a student survey. Then use the words in the box to make statements. If the verb can take both singular and plural forms, write them both.

Why do you study a **foreign language**?	Percentage of students
1. I need to know the language to get a better job. ⟶	85%
2. I want to be able to speak the language when I travel. ⟶	100%
3. I have to study the language because it's a required subject. ⟶	30%
4. I need to be able to read literature in the language. ⟶	0%
5. I study the language because I enjoy it. ⟶	50%

all	half	majority	minority	none

1. need to know the language to get a better job

   A majority of the students needs/need to know the language to get a better job.

2. want to be able to speak the language when they travel

   _____

3. have to study the language because it's a required subject

   _____

4. need to be able to read literature in the language

   _____

5. study the language because they enjoy it

   _____

③ VOCABULARY

Complete the conversations by using the correct form of the expressions in the box.
Make any necessary changes to the expressions.

> have a sharp tongue
> have a way with words
> love to hear oneself talk
> stick to the point
> talk behind someone's back
> talk someone into something
> talk someone's ear off

1. A: I really liked what Justin said about working together as a team.

   B: I agree. It was very inspiring. He really _has a way with words_.

2. A: Did Peter say anything about me after I left?

   B: No. He'd never _____. He'd tell you directly.

3. A: Did you tell Lisa about our plans for her birthday?

   B: I tried to, but she just kept _____ about her problems
   with her car.

4. A: Ms. Jones read my report and said awful things about it.

   B: Well, she _____, but she's also very perceptive.
   Just try to focus on what she's saying about your work.

5. A: I know you want to continue discussing the report, but I'd like to talk about
   my new customer.

   B: Let's _____. We can talk about that later.

6. A: That meeting was so long! I thought Bob would never stop talking!

   B: He sure _____, doesn't he?

7. A: Are you going to the company picnic this weekend?

   B: Well, I wasn't planning to, but Kelly convinced me to go. She knows how to
   _____ I don't want to do!

④ GRAMMAR

Complete these sentences with your own ideas. Use verbs in the present.

1. Each language in the world _is unique._

2. All bilingual people _____

3. Every one of my classmates _____

4. The majority of celebrities _____

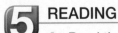

5 READING

A Read the article. Find the words in boldface that match these definitions.

1. form an idea of ___conceptualize___

2. researches _____

3. incredible _____

4. only _____

5. indicate _____

6. native _____

Does the language you speak change the way you think?

Do people who speak different languages actually think differently, or are the 7,000 languages in the world just different means for expressing a universal human way of thinking? To answer that question, linguist Lera Boroditsky **surveys** differences between languages across a number of fundamental categories, including how speakers of different languages **conceptualize** space and time, and how they think about gender.

Regarding spatial orientation, she says, "There are some languages that don't use words like 'left' and 'right.' Instead, everything in the language is laid out in absolute space. That means you have to say things like, 'There is an ant on your northwest leg.'"

The language of the Kuuk Thaayore, an **aboriginal** group in Australia, works like that. Boroditsky's research has shown that the unique way they think about space also affects the way they think about time. Whereas English speakers tend to conceptualize time as running from left to right, the Kuuk Thaayore visualize it from east to west.

Then there is gender. Some languages, like Hebrew, **mark** gender for both people and objects, while Finnish has almost no gender information at all. "English," says Boroditsky, "is somewhere in the middle."

Boroditsky explains the degree to which a language emphasizes gender in its grammatical structure actually affects the way speakers think. She cites a study by Alexander Guiora, who looked at kids learning Hebrew, Finnish, and English as their first language. He asked them, "Are you a boy or a girl?" and had all kinds of clever ways of figuring out how aware they were of their gender. What he found was that kids in these three groups figure it out at different rates. The Hebrew-speaking kids got it first, then the English-speaking kids, and the Finnish-speaking kids last.

These are just a few examples of the **mind-bending** differences Boroditsky has found. She also talks about how the language you speak affects the way you look at colors and changes the way you think about the relationship between cause and effect.

As to the main question – does language affect the way people think – Boroditsky's answer is a clear "yes." At the same time, she allows that language is not the **sole** determinant of thought. "Language shapes thought, and also the way that we think importantly shapes the way we talk," she says, "and aspects of culture importantly shape aspects of language. It's a bi-directional cycle."

B Are the statements true (*T*), false (*F*), or is the information not given (*NG*) in the article? Write the correct letters.

_____ 1. Boroditsky believes that language does affect thinking.

_____ 2. All languages indicate gender in the same way.

_____ 3. Most of the aboriginal languages in Australia conceptualize space and time in similar ways.

_____ 4. Boroditsky believes that language is not the only thing that influences thought.

EXCEPTIONAL PEOPLE
LESSON A ▶ *High achievers*

1 VOCABULARY

Choose the words that best complete the sentences.

1. The *coolheaded* / *soft-hearted* athlete was able to score despite the noisy crowd.

2. I'm so *absent-minded* / *hardheaded* that, after staying up late to finish my paper on time, I forgot to bring it to class!

3. Sam is the kindest and most *cold-blooded* / *warm-hearted* guy I know.

4. Although Emily appears to be silly and *narrow-minded* / *empty-headed,* she's actually quite intelligent.

5. Ethan is *hardheaded* / *hot-blooded.* Once he makes up his mind, he doesn't change.

6. I hope Zach is *cold-hearted* / *open-minded* about our idea. He isn't always willing to consider new approaches to solving problems.

7. My cousins are so *narrow-minded* / *soft-hearted* when it comes to music. They won't listen to anything except jazz.

8. The *cold-hearted* / *absent-minded* killer was sentenced to life in prison.

2 GRAMMAR

Rewrite these sentences using compound adjectives to replace the words in boldface. Sometimes more than one answer is possible.

1. The famous conductor is **recognized by many people**.
   The famous conductor is widely recognized.

2. In my opinion, the politician's speech was **too long**.
   _____

3. Nicole is a model **with curly hair and brown eyes**.
   _____

4. Alyssa is a **very relaxed** boss. She lets employees choose their hours.
   _____

5. Maxwell's is not a restaurant **that many people know about**.
   _____

6. Dr. Kendall's lectures really **make us think about things**.
   _____

7. Katy made a good impression at the interview because she was **dressed so well**.
   _____

What qualities should these people have? Write a sentence using two compound adjectives.

elementary school teacher

mountain climber

1. *An elementary school teacher should be kind-hearted and well educated.*

2. _____

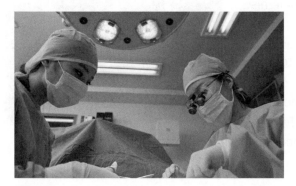

surgeon

judge

3. _____

4. _____

salesperson

soccer player

5. _____

6. _____

4 WRITING

A Read this biographical profile of composer and conductor Leonard Bernstein. Answer the questions below.

LEONARD BERNSTEIN

LEONARD BERNSTEIN was perhaps the single greatest figure in American classical music in the twentieth century. Born in 1918 in Lawrence, Massachusetts, he studied piano as a child in Boston. ❶ Upon his graduation from Harvard University in 1939, he moved to Philadelphia to study at the Curtis Institute. ❷ By the time Bernstein finished his training, he was widely respected as a major talent in the music world. ❸

In 1943, Bernstein became the assistant conductor of the New York Philharmonic. One night, he was asked to substitute for a conductor who was sick. This was a particularly difficult concert, but Bernstein performed brilliantly and was a great success. ❹ Over the next 15 years, he held conducting positions in several of the great orchestras of the world, and he performed as a guest conductor with many others. His work included both live concerts and recordings. ❺

In 1958, Bernstein became the music director of the New York Philharmonic. That same year, he started a series of televised programs called *Young People's Concerts*, designed to teach children an appreciation for great music. At the Philharmonic, Bernstein was a very popular conductor. He brought new music to the orchestra and revitalized older music that hadn't been played for some time.

❻ Bernstein died in New York City in 1990. He conducted and composed music up until the time of his death. Through his lifetime of conducting, composing, teaching, and helping people understand music, he left a great gift to the world.

1. In what year did Leonard Bernstein leave Harvard University? _____

2. How long did Bernstein conduct orchestras all over the world before he became the music director of the New York Philharmonic? _____

3. In what year did Bernstein start *Young People's Concerts*? _____

B There are six numbered circles in the biographical profile. Find where each of the following sentences should go, and write the number of the circle next to the sentence.

_____ a. In 1969, Bernstein left the New York Philharmonic and spent the remaining years of his life composing a wide variety of music, conducting all over the world, and teaching young musicians.

_____ b. At 17, he entered Harvard University, where he studied composition.

_____ c. During his years there, he spent his summers at the Boston Symphony Orchestra's institute at Tanglewood, where he studied with the conductor Serge Koussevitzky.

C Choose someone you admire who has made a difference in people's lives. Research the key facts of the person's life, and write a biographical profile with an introduction and at least two other paragraphs.

GRAMMAR

Read the text and underline the superlative compound adjectives.

Without a doubt, <u>my most fondly remembered</u> teacher is Mr. Hill, my college French professor. He was the most kind-hearted man, and he always showed concern for his students. He went out of his way to make us feel comfortable in class, so we never felt too nervous or anxious to participate. He was the hardest-working teacher I've ever had, and he would always come up with creative ways to help us understand the most difficult lessons. Mr. Hill truly loved French culture, so the cultural lessons were the most thought-provoking of all my classes. He made me feel that I was looking through a window into another world, and he made me want to be a part of that world. I'm afraid I don't remember much French now – it's not the most easily retained language, especially if you don't use it often – but I did learn how great a teacher can be and how rewarding it can be to learn about another culture.

GRAMMAR

Read these conversations and fill in the blank with the superlative form of the adjectives in parentheses.

1. Kay: What did you think about the president's speech?

   Mindy: I thought it was *the most thought-provoking* (thought-provoking) speech she's ever given.

2. Sung: Don't you think Tom is a good cook?

   Nate: Definitely. His paella was ＿＿＿＿＿＿＿＿＿＿＿＿ (great-tasting) dish I've had in a long time!

3. Oscar: What did you think of the lead actor's performance in the movie we saw last night?

   Valerie: I thought he was terrific. He gave one of ＿＿＿＿＿＿＿＿＿＿＿＿ (heartbreakingly convincing) performances in the movie.

4. Rich: Have you seen the video of the singing dog?

   Linda: No, I haven't. But I've heard that it's ＿＿＿＿＿＿＿＿＿＿＿＿ (widely downloaded) clip of the week.

5. Tai: Cory is always so kind to people!

   Sarah: I agree. He's probably ＿＿＿＿＿＿＿＿＿＿＿＿ (warm-hearted) person I've ever met.

6. Brad: How was your trip to Morocco? Were you able to visit the desert?

   Nora: Oh, I was. It was one of ＿＿＿＿＿＿＿＿＿＿＿＿ (breathtakingly beautiful) things I saw on my entire trip!

3 VOCABULARY

Correct the underlined mistake in each sentence with one of the words in the box.
Some words will be used more than once.

after	on	to	through	with

1. I always look <u>through</u> my older sister for fashion advice. _____ *to* _____
2. I know coping with a broken arm is difficult, but just be patient and you'll get <u>after</u> it. _____
3. I'm not sure who to side <u>to</u> in this argument! You both have valid points. _____
4. Many middle-aged people not only look <u>with</u> their children, but they take care of their elderly parents at the same time. _____
5. Who do you take <u>through</u> more, your mother or your father? _____
6. I have very high expectations for myself, and I get frustrated when I don't live up <u>on</u> them. _____
7. Excuse me while I check <u>after</u> the baby. I think I just heard her cry. _____
8. If you don't face up <u>with</u> your problems soon, they'll only get worse. _____

4 GRAMMAR

Use the cues to write sentences that are true for you.
Use superlative compound adjectives in your sentences.

1. incredibly talented actress I can think of
   The most incredibly talented actress I can think
   of is Scarlett Johansson.

2. action-packed movie I've ever seen
   _____
   _____

3. time-saving invention I use
   _____
   _____

4. easily learned subject I've studied
   _____
   _____

5. well-intentioned person I've met
   _____
   _____

6. physically demanding sport I know
   _____
   _____

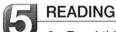
A Read this article about the Awesome Foundation. Choose the adjectives that best describe the organization.

☐ 1. old-fashioned ☐ 3. highly structured ☐ 5. nontraditional
☐ 2. loosely organized ☐ 4. crowdsourced ☐ 6. widespread

TINY GRANTS KEEP "awesome" IDEAS COMING

It was down to two finalists: a woman who wanted to buy a couple of goats to rent out as urban lawnmowers, and a sculptor who wanted to buy a portable welder so he could go around and fix his city. They were both awesome ideas, the trustees agreed, but only one of them could win money that month. And so they had to ask the ultimate question: Which idea was more awesome?

This is the basic premise behind the Awesome Foundation, which is not an actual foundation. It is more like a support group for good ideas. It began in Cambridge, Massachusetts, in 2009, when a group of tech-savvy twenty-somethings, frustrated by the bureaucracy of traditional funding, got together and, in essence, said, "You know what would be awesome? If there were an organization that gave you money if you had an awesome idea." Then they became that organization, loosely.

It works like this: Ten trustees each kick in $100 a month, and together they review the submissions. The winner is given $1,000 for the project, with no strings attached.

The idea is so simple that it has multiplied organically and become a new nonprofit model for the crowdsourcing generation. Today there are more than 20 chapters around the world. Anyone can start one, and the only real rule is that there is no definition for "awesome." That's for each trustee to decide.

The concept of a small grant, handed out by individuals, means the idea has a built-in lightness, according to Tim Hwang, who conceived of the Awesome Foundation shortly after he graduated from college. But there is a recurring bent toward socially conscious public projects. Christina Xu, one of the original trustees who had become frustrated with the failings of traditional nonprofits, says that she "realized maybe the Awesome Foundation was an answer" to that problem.

That may be a reach, but it's indicative of what attracts people to the Awesome Foundation – the belief that ordinary people can create positive change outside of the establishment.

In the end, the trustees unanimously chose the sculptor. They had questions about the goats, but there was no question that the sculptor's idea was awesome.

B Choose the statements that can be confirmed in the article.

☐ 1. Trustees generally fund Awesome awards with their own money.

☐ 2. Traditional nonprofit organizations admire the foundation's work.

☐ 3. There are no rules on who can set up a branch of the Awesome Foundation in a new city.

☐ 4. The foundation has funded thousands of projects around the world.

☐ 5. The foundation consciously avoids strictly defining what should be considered "awesome."

 VOCABULARY

Choose the words that best complete the sentences.

1. I would rather work *around* / *for* a boss who is organized and strict than a boss who is disorganized and nice.

2. Janelle worked *off* / *on* some of her debt to her cousin by designing and managing the website for his business.

3. Showing up late for appointments can work *against* / *toward* you if you are trying to start a new business.

4. If we don't find a way to work *toward* / *around* this problem, we'll never make our deadline.

5. The more people we have working *for* / *on* the report, the faster we'll get it done.

6. Jesse is working *off* / *toward* a degree in marketing and finance.

GRAMMAR

Read each sentence and then answer the questions with *yes* or *no*.

Had Natalie not lost her job at a bakery, she would never have considered starting her own business.

1. Did Natalie lose her job at the bakery? _____*Yes*_____

2. Did she consider starting her own business? _____

Should Natalie's business continue to grow, she might hire another baker.

3. Is Natalie's business growing? _____

4. Has she hired another baker yet? _____

Had Natalie raised a large family, she might not have been able to spend a lot of time developing her business.

5. Was she able to spend a lot of time developing the business? _____

6. Did she raise a large family? _____

Natalie's Cookies might not have become the best-selling cookies in the city had she not worked so hard.

7. Did Natalie's Cookies become the best-selling cookies in the city? _____

8. Did Natalie work hard? _____

3 GRAMMAR

Complete the sentence for each situation using a conditional clause with *Had . . . not . . . .*

1. __*Had*__ the woman __*not answered the ad*__, she'd never have become a veterinary assistant.

2. _____ the couple _____, they wouldn't have had so many kittens at home.

3. _____ the man _____, he wouldn't have won first prize.

4. _____ the woman _____, she wouldn't have started her own business.

5. _____ the man _____, he would never have been served.

6. _____ the woman _____, she wouldn't have bought her new laptop.

A Read this formal letter. Three sentences do not belong because they are too personal or irrelevant. One has already been crossed out. Cross out the other two.

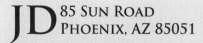 85 SUN ROAD
PHOENIX, AZ 85051

June 7, 2014

Ms. Rosa Marquez
4226 E. 22nd St.
Phoenix, AZ 85016

Dear Ms. Marquez:

I am writing in response to the advertisement for a social media marketer in last week's edition of *Career Focus E-News Digest*. I am very interested in the position and am enclosing my résumé for your consideration. ~~It is very kind of you to read this letter.~~

I believe you will find that I meet all of the qualifications that you specify. In fact, you have probably never had a candidate as qualified as I am! I have had two years of experience as a social media marketing intern at a major nonprofit. Although this was an unpaid position, it gave me valuable experience in managing social media accounts, creating content, and working with analytics.

Additionally, I enjoy working as part of a team and am very good with people. None of my current colleagues wants me to leave.

I would appreciate the opportunity to discuss this position with you in person. I look forward to hearing from you at your convenience.

Sincerely,

James Ditzler
James Ditzler

B Imagine a job that you would be interested in having. Make notes on the following.

Why you want the position:

_____

_____

Your experience:

_____

_____

Why you should be considered:

_____

_____

C Use your notes to write a formal letter applying for the job you are interested in.

GRAMMAR

Choose the expressions that best complete the sentences.

1. *Assuming that / Provided that* I were required to travel for a job, I would turn it down because I don't like to fly.

2. *On the condition that / Whether or not* we continued to get more business, we would have to move to bigger offices anyway.

3. *Whether or not / Provided that* an applicant had the right job skills, I'd definitely hire him or her.

4. *Supposing that / Provided that* your boss wanted to transfer you to another department, how would you feel about it?

5. *Assuming that / Whether or not* you have a good reason to change jobs, I'd strongly recommend staying at your present company.

GRAMMAR

Respond to what the first speaker says in the conversations. Write sentences using the adverb clauses of condition provided.

1. A: If I were offered an interesting job that paid well, I would accept it. (provided that)

   B: *I would probably accept it, too, provided that the benefits were also good.*

2. A: If I had to commute to work on a daily basis, I would definitely do it. It can't be that much of an inconvenience. (on the condition that)

   B: _____

   _____

3. A: If I didn't receive a raise within the first year I worked at a job, I'd leave it and find a new job. (assuming that)

   B: _____

   _____

4. A: Under no circumstances would I ever accept a demotion. No one should move down in a company. (supposing that)

   B: _____

   _____

5. A: If my boss said something in a meeting that I strongly disagreed with, I would definitely speak up. (whether or not)

   B: _____

   _____

6. A: I think that it's OK to lend a family member a large amount of money in order to help them start a business. (provided that)

   B: _____

   _____

3 GRAMMAR

Under what conditions would you do or not do these things? Write sentences using the expressions in the box.

| assuming (that) | on the condition (that) | provided (that) | supposing (that) | whether or not |

1. take a pay cut

   I'd take a pay cut on the condition I were given
   more interesting projects at work.

2. work every weekend

   _____

   _____

3. agree to be transferred to a different country

   _____

   _____

4. work two jobs at the same time

   _____

   _____

5. quit your job and go back to school

   _____

   _____

4 VOCABULARY

Choose the quality that you consider to be the most important for each job.
Then write a sentence explaining why.

1. doctor (leadership ability / training)

   Training is most important for doctors because people's lives are in their hands.

2. artist (self-discipline / initiative)

   _____

3. politician (charisma / influence)

   _____

4. teacher (communication skills / leadership ability)

   _____

5. writer (initiative / training)

   _____

6. business executive (influence / leadership ability)

   _____

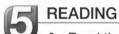

5 READING

A Read the article quickly and answer the questions.

1. What percentage of employees report being truly engaged in their work? _____

2. How many companies does the author say completely meet his criteria? _____

The Twelve Attributes of a
TRULY GREAT PLACE TO WORK

More than 100 studies have found that the most engaged employees – those who report they're fully invested in their jobs and committed to their employers – are significantly more productive, drive higher customer satisfaction, and outperform those who are less engaged. But only 20 percent of employees around the world report that they're fully engaged at work. So, what's the solution? The answer is that great employers must shift the focus from trying to get more out of people to investing more in them by addressing their four core needs – physical, emotional, mental, and spiritual – so they're freed, fueled, and inspired to bring the best of themselves to work every day.

Think for a moment about what would make you feel most excited to get to work in the morning and most loyal to your employer. The sort of company I have in mind would:

1 Commit to paying every employee a living wage. No employee working full time should receive a sum that falls below the poverty line.

2 Give all employees a stake in the company's success. If the company does well, all employees should share in the success in meaningful ways.

3 Design working environments that are safe, comfortable, and appealing to work in. In offices, include a range of physical spaces that allow for privacy, collaboration, and simply hanging out.

4 Provide healthy, high-quality food at the lowest possible prices.

5 Create places for employees to rest and renew during the course of the working day and encourage them to take intermittent breaks.

6 Offer a well-equipped gym and other facilities that encourage employees to move and stay fit.

7 Define clear and specific expectations for what success looks like in any given job. Then treat employees as adults by giving them as much autonomy as possible.

8 Institute two-way performance reviews so that employees not only receive regular feedback about how they're doing but also have the chance to provide feedback to their supervisors.

9 Hold leaders and managers accountable for treating all employees with respect and care.

10 Create policies that encourage employees to set aside time to focus without interruption on their most important priorities.

11 Provide employees with ongoing opportunities and incentives to learn, develop, and grow.

12 Stand for something. Create products, provide services, or serve causes that add value in the world, making it possible for employees to feel good about the companies for which they work.

I've yet to come across a company that meets the full range of their people's needs in all the ways I've described. How about you?

B Answer the following questions with information from the article.

1. What are some of the benefits of having engaged employees?

_____

2. According to the author, what are the four core needs of employees?

_____

3. How does the author think office environments can be made more appealing?

_____

4. According to the article, how does a two-way performance review work?

_____